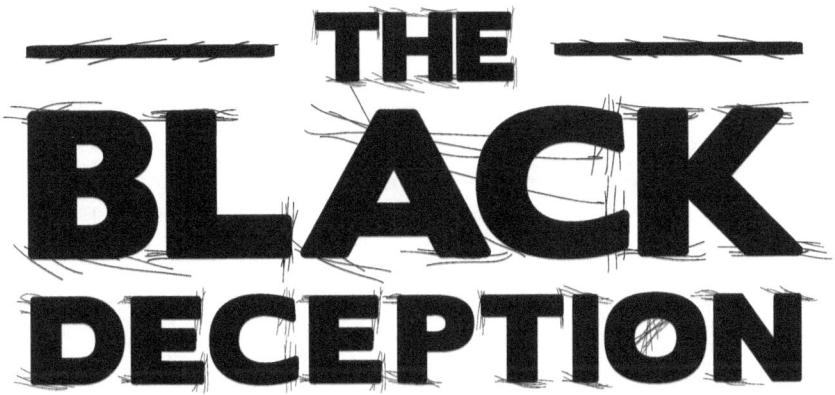

THE BLACK DECEPTION

As We Are Many Wonderful Shades of Brown,
Why Do We Paint Ourselves with a Black Face?

J. LAMAR HATCHETT

LifeRich Publishing is a registered trademark of The Reader's Digest Association, Inc.

LifeRich Publishing books may be ordered through booksellers or by contacting:

LifeRich Publishing
1663 Liberty Drive
Bloomington, IN 47403
www.liferichpublishing.com
1 (888) 238-8637

Because of the dynamic nature of the Internet, any web addresses or links contained in this book may have changed since publication and may no longer be valid. The views expressed in this work are solely those of the author and do not necessarily reflect the views of the publisher, and the publisher hereby disclaims any responsibility for them.

Any people depicted in stock imagery provided by Getty Images are models, and such images are being used for illustrative purposes only. Certain stock imagery © Getty Images.

ISBN: 978-1-4897-1705-4 (sc)
ISBN: 978-1-4897-1706-1 (e)

Library of Congress Control Number: 2018905001

Print information available on the last page.

LifeRich Publishing rev. date: 5/04/2018

Acknowledgements

I would be remiss if I didn't take a moment to recognize some of the people who have had a profound influence on my life and philosophy. These people teach with a purpose as well as by example. This writing would be incomplete without the wisdom that they have imparted.

Crystal H, Larry R, Rufus N, Ruby H, Lovell H, Jesse D, Ivan H, Tom C, MLK Jr.

And my big-hearted sister Susan Williams

Artwork by Erica & Elizabeth Reedy

Introduction

This book offers a new perspective on and an analysis of the subject of race in America. This modern approach will shed new light on the darkest regions of how and why we believe what we believe about race.

This book will focus on a unique group of Americans who are neither natives nor immigrants. I will refer to them as DOS, descendants of slaves. I will explain the chronology and the methodology they used to shape their culture. Consider this book as an instruction manual that offers solutions to correct a navigational error that has been centuries in the making. This is the story of the altered destiny of a people trapped in what we call *The Black Deception.*

Four hundred years ago, when Africans were kidnapped and brought to the New World in shackles and chains, a new chapter of American terrorism began. Who could have dreamed this New World criminal practice would endure for centuries? Who could have imagined it would shape the culture and destiny of so many all the way to the present day?

I will always refer to this practice as criminal and consider it an affront to the US Declaration of Independence, a foundational document that launched our strong nation and stated all men were created equal and were therefore endowed with certain inalienable rights.

This literary manual is a prescription for a people who have had their destiny violently shifted off course. This is a prescription for what ails the DOS, and it is now available to all who dare to swallow the pill.

Read *The Black Deception*, absorb it, and free yourself from deception. You may be able to serve as a guide. In this book are the tools you will need to disassemble category boxes that contain "us and them." Your life and the example you become can be a roadmap that guides other souls who have not yet realized how far they have drifted from their destiny.

The handbook for healing America's great racial divide.

The Revelation of Proper Destiny

Only the strong survived. The grueling, inhumane voyage slaves endured took as long as four months depending on trade winds, routes, and ports of departure.

Slave traders quickly realized that the mortality rate, which could reach 30 percent, and load factors onboard their ships greatly affected the profitability of the slave trade. The logical, humane thing they could have done was improving the conditions of their cargo—our ancestors—and therefore deliver a greater number of healthy slaves to market. But nothing was humane about the slave trade. Slave traders simply increased the number of slaves they transported. They cruelly crammed their kidnapped victims into ships' bowels. The dead were simply tossed overboard. The men, women, and children too weak to survive the tortuous journey were simply counted as the cost of doing business.

We all know the story of the inhumane slave trade of the American South, but few understand the tragic story of the aftermath. The

Emancipation Proclamation and the Thirteenth Amendment legally ended slavery in the 1860s. We will explore how the four million slaves who had known only cruelty and bondage could survive in a hostile, capitalistic society.

Despite broken promises of reparations by the government, centuries of torture, and economic disenfranchisement, our ancestors emerged from this nightmare ready and able to excel. Men of color, such as Hiram Revels, a political leader, was elected to the US Senate in the decade after slavery ended. Former slaves who dared enter the political arena had only one choice: the Republican Party. All slave owners at the time of the Civil War were Democrats.

Former slaves quickly proved they could be excellent politicians, merchants, teachers, farmers, and businesspeople. They proved to be too good for the likes of some; in many cases, they outperformed their European-American counterparts. The southern Democrats (sore losers) were still busy lynching and intimidating brown-skinned people to hinder their ascendance. The thought of these people once held as chattel succeeding to the utmost degree was more than the ignorant racists' limited intellects could digest.

Our ancestors understood the dignity, honor, and independence of work. They actually excelled at capitalism. After generations spent in bondage, they were determined to prosper if and when they realized their strong hope of freedom.

A group of former slaves and their offspring built a community of commerce and capitalism that was the envy of all who witnessed it. During the late 1970s, I lived in Tulsa, Oklahoma, and I had the privilege to actually meet and talk with some who had lived in this community. This example of socioeconomic excellence could have been crafted only by highly intelligent people—people who had previously been forbidden to read or write by law.

The Greenwood section of Tulsa was a shining example of our ancestors operating without an inferiority complex or interference. The area comprised thirty-five blocks of socioeconomic prosperity. More than ten thousand brown-skinned people lived in a social and economic order enviable even by today's standards. The schools were good, the crime rate was low, and opportunities were abundant. Those who wanted to start businesses raised the money by selling stock to members of the community, who made sure those businesses became successful. These self-sufficient Negroes a hundred years ago were living in the midst of the fiercest racial hatred, but they prospered in spite of that.

If not for a government-involved declaration of war on this advanced community, it may have grown to become the financial capital of the Midwest. Some more-ambitious estimates say that it would have become the economic model for urban America.

There were no government programs to help poor negroes. There were no programs to help underachievers at all. But they did not need help. All they needed was an equal chance to prosper. They knew who they were. They, my friends, were not deceived. Those who settled that community had assimilated into American society in a very pleasing manner. The rates of building, commerce, and expansion were robust!

But why was their community bombed into oblivion? Who interfered with a genuine, American success story?

Greenwood was attacked because racist people practice racism for two reasons: ignorance and fear. Ignorance drove the racists to hate people who looked different even though they were almost genetically identical. Fear caused them to ponder what would become of them if they allowed these brown-skinned people to thrive and prosper at all much less achieve a higher level than the racists were capable of. The racists feared they could not compete, and the fear of losing their dominance drove them to literally drop burning balls of turpentine on Greenwood's rooftops. The goal of this assault, was to wipe an American success story out of existence.

The majority of the DOS today don't know this true story. This community was wiped out of history as well as existence. The newspapers, courts, and insurance companies colluded to cover up this government-sanctioned terrorist attack against American citizens perpetrated on American soil.

Government officials stood idly by as citizens they were sworn to protect were literally firebombed. These same politicians passed laws, including fire codes, stating that no building could be rebuilt on any site that had previously had a building burned down. You heard that right. The racists burned those buildings down, and the same racists passed laws to ensure that there would be no resurrection of prosperity among the DOS community.

I conducted an unscientific survey that led me to believe that less than 15 percent of the US population has any meaningful knowledge of what happened, what this community had been, or the effects this example of pride and excellence had had.

This example of misplaced history is not a lone example or a mere oversight. That is because the victors in any war get to write its history. The southern Democrats and their northern counterparts waged a post-slavery war against the recently freed people. They passed laws and rules designed to keep the recently freed always a step or two behind. In cases where their stealthy legislative warfare failed to slow down our determined ancestors, they resorted to burning, bombing, and lynching. Our ancestors, overwhelmed by the joy of freedom, didn't know how to fight the war until it was over. The victors wrote the history, and that is why so many know so little of the gleaming accomplishments of those recently freed Americans—our ancestors.

The war I speak of was declared by racists who had one goal in mind—to render a people capable of superior achievement a permanent subservient underclass.

News flash! You were never meant to be America's minimum-wage workforce. Brown-skinned people were never destined to be prison fodder or deadbeat dads. The DOS were never meant to be the needy. You, my brothers and sisters, were never meant to accept long-term government assistance to provide for your children. If you think otherwise, you have been deceived. Your legacy of pride and excellence has been stolen. You have been rammed off course on your way to your destiny. Your identity has been so corrupted that you hate those who look like you, and you long for the looks of your deceivers. You kill other brown-skinned men by the thousands each year as proof of your self-loathing. Yes, that's what I said. The murder statistics in Chicago alone are proof that many people hate what they see in the mirror.

The number of murders perpetrated by blacks is seven times higher than the murders perpetrated by nonblacks. Blacks in a deceived state of mind have been committing about half the nation's murders for some time. Ninety percent of blacks murdered in the United States are killed by other blacks.

But there is a cure for what ails them.

Too Much Skin in the Game

Attention—more breaking news—you are not black! Someone told you that black would be your defining call sign from now on and you said okay? Look in the mirror, take this book with you, and go look. You may be blessed with a beautiful shade of brown skin, but you are not black. The term *black* as it is used to define race is not even a statement of skin color; it is a stealthy racial epithet. And its power lies in that stealth.

This one description applied to a group of people has wrought far more damaging consequences than the words *coon*, *nigga*, or *spook* ever could. Ponder the questions in the next paragraph honestly and carefully. Deep inside, you most likely always knew the answers.

Though we are many wonderful shades of brown, why should we insist on painting ourselves in blackface? What are the historical connotations of black? Since it is not an accurate description of our skin color, who decided to put that label on us? Who has the right to define us other than ourselves?

You have heard it all of your life—black people this, black people that, black people don't (fill in the blank), and of course, black men are (fill in the blank again). When you fill in the blanks, they are almost always inferior, negative words.

The Black Deception is a life manual that will help you discover the answers to these and many other crucial questions. As you discover these answers, you will begin to see why so many grovel at the bottom of the barrel in the American socioeconomic order.

Since we all agree that *black* is not an accurate description of skin color, what is it meant to describe? Who created the rule that people who have a brown-skinned, distant relative in their lineage must be considered black? Barack Obama's mother is not black, but he is? Barack has medium-brown skin, he has a white-skinned mother, but he is the first black president. White plus brown equals black? Where is the logic in that?

The answer as to who created the one drop of "black" blood rule is simple. Colonizers and racist needed to maintain control of the population that they had enslaved all while they raped the captive women with impunity. The consequences of their immorality created a legal heirship predicament for the south.

To make sure that the offspring of the rape victims could never be in line to inherit the land, the one drop of black blood rule was used to eliminate the possibility of any such claim, you see once you were **declared black**, (even if your skin color mirrored your white daddy) your human rights could be denied with impunity.

So the question for today is, why should we cling to and accept rules drawn up hundreds of years ago by evil men for evil purposes? I will not accept their rules and neither should you!

In some cultures, children are assumed to be their mothers' ethnicities. This way of thinking makes sense because the ethnicity of the mother is never in doubt. However this was not the case in the south. The rule was instituted to facilitate rape without repercussion. It is foolishness to continue to cooperate and perpetuate a rule whose origin spawns from such evil.

Now go back to your childhood. Reach into your crayon box.

There are only brown and white crayons left. Grab a brown and a white crayon and start coloring and mixing them together. Would your artwork ever turn out to be black? Wouldn't it be just a lighter shade of brown?

Take this example a step further. Your teacher looks at your coloring book and says, "You mixed brown and white. You're a terrible artist. Your pictures are always so black." She would not be referring to your color palette, would she? She would be telling you that your artwork is dark and ugly, that it is negative and inferior in content. If this teacher is someone you respect, her words would have power. If you believe what she teaches, your schema concerning the color brown might be permanently downgraded to something less than desirable, something unacceptable. But a persons schema can, be altered to perceive brown as black—black with all its negative connotations intact.

Here is a question that even the most deceived among us will still know the answer to. Does a greater amount of melanin in your skin limit your academic capabilities, work ethic, or business skills? Does this trace chemical cause men to disrespect women, shoot their brothers, or depend on government programs to support their offspring? I could keep the questions rolling, but I have made my point. Anyone with a fully functioning brain knows that the answer to these silly questions is simply no. An abundance of melanin in your skin is a blessing, not a curse. This substance can create a beautiful skin tone as well as provide built-in UV protection.

Since we all agree that melanin is good for us, there must be another reason for the dismal social economic statistics attributed to black American society today.

Before you grab the low-hanging and much too obvious answer of racism, look back more than a hundred years ago and observe the lives and philosophy of recently freed slaves and their offspring. Authentic history tells a story that is different from the one conventional wisdom portrays. Racism and all its ugliness were in full operation in America. Democratic lawmakers wrote unconstitutional laws, and lynching and other forms of racial intimidation were in full force.

However, even in the midst of intense racism, your ancestors wove a sustainable socioeconomic fabric that rivaled its European counterpart in every aspect. Our ancestors built thriving communities in the face of retaliatory racism. They realized the value of education and excellence, and parents made it the highest of priorities for their children. When racists sought to deny these children higher education, did our ancestors tell their children, "I guess you'll have to work for minimum wage all your life"? Hell no! They got busy laying the foundations of what came to be known as HBCUs—historically black colleges and universities. You are starting to see what today's black generations have lost and that negroes in the late 1800s knew who they were. They had a determination that was not to be denied.

Our ancestors excelled to the point of angering racists into a frenzy. Those frenzies often ended with many proud negroes dead and their communities in smoke and ashes. Well today, there are no burn-it-down, racist, frenzied attacks. The question is, if there were, would they even find any viable targets?

The esteemed Brookings Institute conducted an extensive scientific study of the common factors present in American family poverty. The factors have nothing to do with skin tone. They have everything to do with state of mind and learned behavior. Here they are.

- giving education a low priority
- having children out of wedlock before age twenty-one
- failing to honor and respect full-time work

Is it a surprise to anyone that these three conditions have become synonymous with being black in the inner city? Consider these statistics.

- black high school graduation rate—69%
- black poverty—27%
- black children born out of wedlock—70%
- black unemployment—9%

These high percentages paint a "black" future for many DOS families just as the word *black* is used to describe the plague that swept through Europe in the Middle Ages and the collapse of Wall Street on a certain Tuesday in 1929 that crippled the economy for decades. Black means the absence of light. It also means no light at the end of the tunnel for those trapped in its deception. Should we continue to cooperate and use this moniker of death and destruction as our primary identifying characteristic? Now I present to you this question, was Barak Obama the first "black" president? The answer depends on whether or not you choose to cooperate with evil racist philosophy. Here in lies the truth buried in hundreds of years of deception.

THREE

Taking Control of Race and Racism

Y ou are no more a black than you are a fingernail or a hair. You understand that black is merely a flawed description of skin color. You understand that skin color is useless in determining the true nature of a human. It can't predict anyone's character, compassion, intelligence, or courage. You know that skin color should never be used to categorize humans.

So why is race categorization a mega topic that can dominate the news and social media? To answer this question, you must first understand what race really is and why it exists. Here is a working definition of race that will help you understand America's obsession with the subject: race categorization—a psychological warfare tool created and used by evil men for the express purpose of dividing, conquering, and controlling specific groups of people. Race is truly a rip off of humanity's, humanity.

Why should people want to control other people who don't look like them? Well, all people don't. Most people would be happy to exist in harmony and equality with their fellow human beings. But some humans have twisted schemas and bent psyches. They mistakenly believe that skin tone alone has the power to make one superior or inferior. We shall refer to these poor, demented people as racists.

Racist are spiritual garbage cans polluted with fear and ignorance. Their inner garbage is so voluminous that they feel the need to unload some of it on targets just to feel some relief. But don't hate racists—do not allow their garbage to pollute your soul. You must maintain your superior mind-set over racists. You can defeat racists by being smarter, kinder, and more humane. Defeat their garbage by refusing to allow their spiritual soil to dirty you up. Smile at racists when they expose their inferiority by using racial epithets or clichés.

It is not a sign of wisdom or compassion to be angry at those of lesser intellect. To quote the brilliant Marcus Garvey, "Intelligence rules the world and ignorance carries its burden." They are just displaying a weakness of character they learned from people in authority over them. More often than not, those people were their parents. You must never dignify racist remarks with anger; you are above such trifling. The superior response is to have some pity on their ignorant, little minds and move on. Any other response is a descent to their level. Always meet ignorance with the proper response; to do otherwise would be to act out of ignorance yourself.

Should you encounter racism in the workplace, rejoice! Yes, rejoice! The US judicial system has laws to protect its citizens from racial discrimination in the workplace. Record and document all authentic acts of racial discrimination in the workplace. Hire the best attorneys available, and take the racist to the bank. Never lose your cool, and never get angry—just get paid!

It might even be appropriate to say thank you to the racist. Smile as you start your own righteously conducted business using the proceeds from your lawsuit. This is how you fight—with poise and intelligence. This is how you win the psychological war. You win each battle with wise counsel, not with fists or feet. Protesting and marching make the six o'clock news, but lawsuits make you financially whole.

History reveals that racists will target a group of people based on geography, language, or skin color. Once a target is selected, they might use skin color to divide and conquer a strong group of people. This method was used throughout colonialism, and its ramifications continue to fuel conflict among divided people today.

When people look with disdain on others because of minor physical differences, something is wrong. When the thought of someone not looking like you is offensive, something is wrong. When you commit actions to deprive other humans of the rights you hold dear, something is wrong with you. Very wrong. If you are that person, you, my friend, are in the primary stages of mental illness. Yes, that is what I said. Here is how it works.

A human being is an integrated circuit much like a computer. You need hardware, power and software to run a computer. Humans require three similar components—spirit, soul, and body together in one autonomous being. The spirit is the electricity, the soul is the software, and of course the body represents the hardware.

The default settings for human software is consistent for all newborns; the settings are for peace and love. They compel the human to embrace the gregarious nature of harmony. The software flashes an error message when a human is in conflict or solitude. This Integrated circuit that is a human being needs virus protection from malware if it is to function properly.

No one was ever born hating other people. Only when there is a mental short circuit of some kind does such aberrant behavior manifest. Only when files have been corrupted or infected does human behavior become evil. That is when wicked behavior such as racism and murder manifest.

Many examples support this theory. The easiest one to observe is the pure nature of children. They will never reject other children because of differing physical characteristics such as skin tone or hair texture. A childs mental state remains pure and natural until mentally flawed parents', influence infects them. They plant the racism virus in the software of their offspring. There are other examples that mental corruption and racism go hand in hand, but I believe you get the point.

How deep is your love? How much do you love your neighbor, your fellow man? As we continue, you will answer this question. I am asking all who read this life manual to consider this.

History proves that our new definition of racism is correct. We have established that the concept of race categorization was created for evil and selfish purposes. The plague of racial classification was born from a need to justify treating people differently and unfairly to create a second or subclass of people. There are no positive, righteous reasons to use the divide, conquer, and control mechanisms associated with race. As we approach the year 2020, it is time for enlightened Americans to abandon this obsolete stain on humanity.

So, how deep is your love? You will answer this burning question in a moment. Are you ready? I am asking people who love righteousness, who have good in their hearts. I am speaking to you right now! Will you join me in this aspirational goal for the betterment of all who share this planet?

We must formally declare right now the death, deconstruction, and burial of race in our lives by no longer interacting with or judging our fellow humans based on an outdated and evil premise.

Before you become upset concerning the consequences of this declaration, before you start your list of all the wonderful traits and traditions of your ethnicity or culture, let me tell you what this new paradigm does not mean. It does not mean you abandon the righteous gatherings and traditions of your culture. If you are proud of the heritage and good accomplishments of your ancestors, continue to be. If you eat corned beef and cabbage on Saint Patty's day, by all means continue. Chalupas on Cinco de Mayo? Collard greens on Sunday? By all means continue. Keep the beautiful aspects of your culture intact. Share them with everyone; we will all benefit from that expansion and interaction. Rich cultural traditions benefit each generation and create a more eclectic and interesting world.

Racism as it exists today was never meant to be; it was created for egregious purposes by equally egregious people. Today, we as enlightened people reject the concept. We refuse to allow an outdated, evil concept to dictate our lives. We formally and officially declare race dead and humanity alive and well.

We are all members of one master group—humanity. In this group are many language, cultural, and geopolitical differences, but we are all the same people.

If we are not brainwashed or deceived, don't we all want better lives for our children? Don't we all aspire to engage in activities that benefit the pursuit of happiness? Wouldn't we all like to leave this world better off than it was when we entered it? Don't we all eschew war and desire to live in peace? Those who do not embrace these common human factors are creatures of darkness. Their software is about to flash a fatal error message. They are the casualties of psychological warfare they did not know they were engaged in. All humanity shares theses common goals. Only when evil enters people's hearts do they abandon these righteous qualities; only then do they pursue conquest driven by greed and fear.

Lay aside ignorance, fear, and greed. Celebrate the diversity and common goals of humanity. Use this manual to remove the virus from your software.

Always remember that racial categorizations and separation are obsolete tools created by the evil, for inhumane purposes. Here is how we start to change.

FOUR

Practical Steps to Bury Race

1. Teach your children that they are human and that we are all human. We may enjoy various ethnic traditions, but we are all in the singular human race. Refuse to pass on hate and division to the next generation. Allow your children's pure love for humanity to endure.
2. Celebrate and share your positive cultural traditions with all who care to learn and participate in them. We are stronger as a nation for the sharing.
3. Petition our government, hospitals, and institutions to remove and cease and desist from all forms of race data tracking. Until they do, check "other" or "human," or "US citizen," or "American" on any form containing racial interrogatories.
4. We are only a few short years from technology that will breach the language barrier in real time. We will speak and understand all languages. In the meantime, don't let language stop you from appreciating the beauty in diverse cultures.

I challenge you to submit additional practical steps and real-life victory stories of how you stamped out race in your life.

Racial categories should have never been created, and they should no longer exist. Here is a true story that illustrates what I mean.

One Sunday afternoon, I was playing music at Armstrong Park in New Orleans. A group of African-Caribbean drummers met there every Sunday to jam to the beats and rhythms of their ancestors. They invited children and adults to pull up a drum and join them. They taught all to become one with the rhythm.

I joined them with my guitar, and we were deep into the rhythm. All of a sudden, some unexpected visitors arrived—six music students from Paris on vacation and armed with brass. They barely spoke English, and we spoke only a little French. We exchanged pleasantries for a moment until someone shouted out the title of a Louis Armstrong jazz standard. The young Parisians' faces lit up and they shouted "Oui, oui! Yes, we know! Yes, we play!"

For the next two hours, we played as if we had studied a song list together. Tourists and locals gathered by the hundreds to experience the sound. We took turns playing solos. Our harmony was tight. We played as one band. White Europeans and brown-skinned people from as far away as Africa and South America spontaneously united in musical bliss. This makeshift rainbow of colors jammed in the unity of improvisational jazz.

I paused for a moment to take in the sight and sound of it all and knew this was how it was meant to be—French, Africans, Americans, Cubans, and Venezuelans in all of God's wonderful shades speaking the same language of music. When we finished, there was a spontaneous explosion of love as all the musicians hugged each other—we were new friends rejoicing in a day of peace harmony and love. For a time in Armstrong park race did not exist and it was as the lyric of his trademark song "what a wonderful world"!

There is so much to gain from leaving race in the dust of the past. There is nothing to lose when you dare to love people in the complete absence of prejudice.

Another true story comes to mind about a brown skinned route salesman who was transferred to a southern rural area that was teaming with racism and KKK members. The salesman quickly learned that many of his customers not only didn't want to buy from him, they didn't even wish to acknowledge his presence. This individual understood many of the principles outlined in this book, he knew that becoming offended by these mental dwarfs was beneath him and that he would certainly not allow their ignorance to rub off on him. So this man decided to ignore the slurs and insults and render the best service that his route customers had ever experienced. He responded with kindness to the mentally deficient racist for months on end. As the months passed by, his patience started to pay off. One by one his customers (some KKK members) started to respond to his kindness as they came to the inevitable conclusion that he wasn't going anywhere, and he wasn't going to treat them as they had treated him. They started having conversation that was not business related, they spoke of family, politics and sports. He broke the cold hard ice of racism with patience and intelligence. The salesman realized that he had accomplished a good thing and that he was doing a great job developing sales on his route, but he never imagined what was yet to come.

A customer who had been one of the first to accept his kindness made a shocking confession, he told the salesman that he joined the Klan at a young age and had accepted its dogma as truth. He also confessed that something about the Klan doctrine always bothered his conscience. Well to make a long story short this man left the Klan, why, because another man helped him to identify and eliminate a mental dysfunction. One might say that the salesman functioned as a sort of antivirus that identified the files that were corrupted by malware and eliminated the virus. I think that we should refer to the salesman as *Mr. Norton*. A short time later the customer asked the salesman to stop by, because he had something to give him. The salesman stopped in to see what the customer had for him, he was then shocked and blown away as the former Klansman turned over his KKK uniform to his new friend, as a memento to remind him that he was free and clear of his racist past. At last count the salesman has collected a half dozen Klan robes, given to him in the same fashion.

This is a true story, if you would like to read the full account, contact us and we will send it to you as told by the salesman to a popular radio personality. The salesman realized that his enemy was not the Klan member, his enemy was his fear and disbelief that he could not DEFEAT ignorance and racism using the superior tools and tactics that we all have at our disposal. Intelligence, Patience, Love, and Inner Peace. When properly deployed these weapons defeat ignorance, evil and racism EVERYTIME.

You have seen the bumper sticker that reads Erase Racism. Now. Let's do that!

FIVE

Statements of Clarification Concerning Race

I will clarify two points I may have taken for granted while writing this manual. The diversity of schema (mind-sets) of the millions of readers who study this book is immeasurable and makes clarification a necessity.

First, when I call for a special love in the DOS community, that is not a mandate for brown people to love others any less. This appeal is an outright request to honor and cherish the common past and valiant struggles of our ancestors. The call for a special love is also a request to shake off the inferiority complex that plagues so many who don't understand why they do what they do, why they fear the sun might make them darker, or why they think straight hair is good hair. I guess the beauty gods must have told them that curly hair was bad hair! This special love is not about thinking less of others but about embracing your own distinguishing characteristics and heritage.

Second, when this manual teaches you to love and forgive all who have wronged you, it is for your benefit, not theirs. You will also learn that racism is not the enemy. We readily acknowledge the evil nature and the hostile intent of racists.

What we refuse to acknowledge, however, is that we do not possess the power to rise above it. It is our responsibility to use our intellect, character, and nobility to deny racism the power to impede our progress. We do not absolve racists of their sins; they should repent for their own sakes. I pray that they would have a change of mindset.

When we understand that we control our destinies, we have no need to play the victim card. When we win, we will enjoy the spoils of victory.

Stop Giving Away Your Power

Every time you hear someone of color make one the following statements, you have just witnessed the abdication of power. If these statements are in your repertoire, get rid of them. If you have friends who use them, help them to stop.

- I am black, so I can't find a job.
- I have a criminal record, so I can't get a job.
- I call myself and my friends "black niggas."
- I can't compete due to white privilege.
- I know they will not let me achieve this or that.

Each time you give in to these clichés, you lose power. Stop worrying about white privilege and start exercising your inherent inner strength. Decide to achieve something great with the attitude that no one can stop you from doing that.

We will refer to this power as inner strength. White privilege on some level does exist, and the only tool in your arsenal to combat it is your inner strength that tells you, *I'm going to win anyway. If I have to work twice as hard, twice as long, I'll get mine. I will excel and become and expert. I will become too valuable to resist.* Inner strength, my brothers and sisters, is why we excel in sports. It is now time to apply this inner strength to education, business, and humanitarianism.

The black deception has caused too many to believe that preparation is distasteful and should be avoided. Not cool. This attitude has become a curse passed from deceived black parents to their offspring. The deceived mind-set has caused soaring high school dropout rates and low post-secondary education participation. The deceived mind will always find an excuse for low achievement that does not require introspection.

By most socioeconomic metrics, the DOS lag far behind their European-descended counterparts. The history of institutional racism in America prior to 1970 dealt a powerful blow to the aspirations of many. Racism still exists in American culture on many levels. Some believe it will be with us well into the future. With that thought in mind, let us shift from what has happened to us and examine what can happen for us. Let us direct our attention to how we respond to and rise above racism. Let us concentrate on how we can eliminate and mitigate its consequences.

You possess the power to defeat racism's ability to stifle your success. I don't care if you have been told you don't have it by people you respect, admire, love, and look up to. A wise proverb states that if the blind lead the blind, they will both fall in a ditch. A slightly more appropriate proverb for our purposes is, "If the deceived follow the deceived, the deception becomes self-perpetuating."

When the deception becomes self-perpetuating, the deceivers win! You, my, friend may have become an accomplice of the racists and are aiding and abetting in your destruction. But there is a cure for what ails you. Let us examine the path to wellness.

SEVEN

Let's All Get Well

The first step in mitigating the ability of racism to alter your destiny is to realize and accept this fact—the enemy is not the racist system; it is your failure to understand that you possess the power and intellect to overcome the racist system.

The civil rights movement with all its genuine effort and righteous intentions was not enough. More than fifty years of legislation, marches, debates, and threats of boycotts have not cleared the fog of deception. The disparities in the areas of wealth, home ownership, education, imprisonment, crime, and murder rates have not shown significant improvement. In some of these areas, the statistics are worsening.

The time has come for an enhanced approach. All American citizens inherit civil rights. The issue for many DOS in American society today is not so much civil rights but rather inner rights—the belief that we can and should aspire and achieve the best. The tragic consequences of allowing our enemies to define us must stop.

The daily news is a constant reminder that black crime, education, income, housing, and family structures are inferior. It is time to shed the underachiever label society has branded us with. It is time to draw upon our inner rights!

Our inner rights give us the ability to access who and what we are as individuals free from definitions, stereotypes, and others' low expectations. Our inner rights give us freedom to express our gifts and talents to their maximum potential.

I have interviewed, questioned, and employed thousands of DOS in my life. I have gazed into the hopeless eyes of men who believe they will never make more than $15 per hour. Men with children to support. Men who failed to prepare themselves to excel in a capitalist society. They pin their hopes on the government raising the minimum wage. These men are oblivious to the fact that the minimum-wage worker is still on the bottom regardless of how high they raise the rate. What is it about the word *minimum* they don't understand?

I have asked some men wearing pants six inches below their waists why they did that. I have never had an answer that was original, individual. Their answers were the result of the herd mentality. They didn't really have a reason. It was just what they did.

I have gazed into the lovely brown eyes of beautiful young sisters who have fallen into the trap of poverty. They have failed to prepare to enter a gainful profession, they have children too young, and they have no men committed to them or their children. Their responses are a bit more colorful than those of the men, but in the final analysis, they also are simply following the herd.

Unfortunately, civil rights will not deliver these people from their misery. Congress can pass no law that will alter their life circumstances. It is time to introduce and awaken these people to their inner rights.

The definition of insanity is the repeating the same action and expecting different results. Let us examine our current murder, unemployment, poverty, and imprisonment rates. It would be insane of us to not try a different approach to these problems. Let us focus on our God-given abilities to be innovative, smart, and noble human beings.

Your enemy is not a racist system; your enemy is your failure to realize **you** possess the power to overcome that system. Say that over and over until hundreds of years of brainwashing have been erased and you believe it. Don't let anyone tell you it's not that simple.

You learned to dismiss your greatness. You learned to disrespect your women. You learned to become what your enemy has defined you to be. You learned to embrace your enemy's racial slurs as a badge of honor. I remind you that Snoop once said he was a "real nigga," and some even applauded. You have even learned to believe you are a victim of white society in need of government programs to survive.

You have abandoned your right to bring out that unique, creative individual you are and your right to not follow the herd. You will relearn what comes naturally to you. You can and will accept your true heritage. Tap into your inbred potential for greatness. Your ancestors endowed you with a superior moral character and a love for all people. You possess great intellect and imagination and can dominate any field you are called to.

Do you have the courage? Yes, you do. Your ancestors passed it on to you. You see, without superior determination and courage, they would not have survived. As you know, many did not survive the brutal journey to America, but you are the descendant of survivors, the toughest of the tough. You are the prodigy of determined overcomers. Take the courage inside you and dare to step into your true destiny at the pinnacle of society and success. Take the steps, use the methods, follow the prescription at the end of this manual, and you will heal!

Have you ever googled "famous black inventors"? Have you ever wondered why 90 percent of them died more than fifty years ago? George Washington Carver, Louis Latimer, Percy Julian—the list of great black innovators and trailblazers is too long for this book to acknowledge. These people are your ancestors who exhibited superior intelligence and determination in the most hostile environments. They had a will to succeed that even the fiercest racism could not quench.

Our ancestors imagined prosperity and a better life. They went to work and made it happen. Your ancestors passed these qualities down to you, but deceived minds have trouble accessing those files.

A friend of mine who happens to be of European ancestry told me that America would be one big cultural bore if it were not for the contributions of your ancestors. He highlighted everything from jazz to rock 'n' roll and high fives to cool greetings. He said that the great colloquial phrases came from our ancestors. He carried on about the dominance of Jim Brown and the grace of Muhammad Ali, the creativity and skill of Michael Jordan and Magic Johnson. He told me not to leave out the pure musical genius of Miles, Quincy, Michael, and Prince. He drove home his point with this: "Without the contribution of the DOS, America would be plain old white bread with no butter, no flava." Yes, he did say "flava"!

People who make up no more than 13 percent of the population have had an overwhelming influence on and have delivered major contributions to American culture. They were a people seemingly banished to a permanent, second-class place. They faced every stumbling block imaginable. They were shackled by a separate and unequal education system and government-sanctioned attacks, lynchings, and burnings. Yet they still heavily influenced the culture, music, art, and soul of this nation. I guess this is what Ms. Angelou meant when she penned the words "and still I rise, I rise, I rise."

Fellow descendants, the time has come to acknowledge something deep in us that refuses to go unnoticed. A flame is burning in us that even the icy-cold waters of racism cannot extinguish.

The only way racists had to slow down this freight train of integrity, intellect, and creative talent was to derail your true identity and give you a new one. The new identity says that you follow, that you do not lead. The new identity says that you are not a provider, that you need the government to provide for you. This new identity is devoid of light. It is angry, violent, calamitous, unethical … Hold on! This new identity sounds a lot like the *Webster's* dictionary definition of "black."

EIGHT

The Virtue of the Pre-Black Era vs. the Decadence of the Post-Black Era

"Negro" was more or less a scientific racial category. However, "black" was a label with a purpose. You are what you believe you are. The Bible says we are what our hearts tell us we are.

The black label with all its dreadful connotations came crashing down on the heads of a once proud and respectful people. A 1968 scientific poll concluded that 70 percent of the DOS would rather be referred to as negro instead of black; it seemed "negro" would remain the reference label of choice. This historical fact leads one to ponder just who hung the black label around the necks of the DOS population in the US. Well, the black (label) megatrend gained a full head of steam, and the change was official by the mid-1970s.

The southern Democrats had lost their legislative grip on racial suppression. The law of the land was now equality. No longer could they openly discriminate and suppress a people without consequences.

There was no legal way to stop brown-skinned people from achieving their highest goals and aspirations.

Brown-skinned Americans had a legal path and right to pursue the American dream. Our ancestors had done this in Greenwood, Rosewood, and other communities established by former slaves. The modern judicial system in the US would no longer just stand by and watch jealous racists burn down whole communities. At last, there was only one thing that could stifle the achievements of these proud survivors.

That one thing was the loss of their identity, the loss of that common bond and legacy that had sustained hope and dignity though the decades. The often persecuted but never defeated negroes changed their identity.

I loved James Brown as a musician and activist. He meant well. Stokely Carmichael meant well also. One hot summer during the turmoil of the civil rights era, they penned the song and the chant "Say it loud—I'm black and I'm proud!" And who can forget "Ungawa! Black power!"?

Before any of you JB/SC fans jump on me, slow your roll. I readily acknowledge what they meant to convey and how they wanted to inspire a people. I agree in principle with what they wanted to accomplish. For a brief time, something wonderful occurred. There was unity around a message. There was even pride around the message. That message had skin color as a driving philosophy. But the skin-color description was not even anatomically correct, and that was the fatal and destructive flaw in the message. Yes, fatal and destructive. This study is an attempt to unwind and demystify what was so wrong with this particular choice of a unifying call to action.

We will now examine characteristics and trends in general, before we were black and after that. Resist the temptation to point out exceptions, and look at the overall pattern and direction, which are extremely negative.

Pre-Black: Virtues

- stronger work ethic
- high rates of marriage and family stability
- high priority placed on education and the rise of HBCUs
- more community-owned businesses
- great respect for life
- high levels of creativity and ingenuity
- high levels of moral philosophy and optimism

Post-Black: Deficiencies

- pervasive victim mentality
- acceptance of the government-messiah syndrome
- low educational expectations and a decline of HBCUs
- tolerance of self-destructive behavior (B2B murder rates)
- 13 percent of the population committing 51 percent of US homicides (90 percent B2B)
- blatant disrespect for our women
- acceptance of a high unemployment rate
- low work-ethic reputation
- the absent-father syndrome
- lukewarm aspirations

A prominent hip-hop artist referred to himself as a real "nigga"; that man has accepted a derogatory description of himself. In my opinion, he has mentally surrendered to the deception. The deception of your deceivers is completed by our use of such epithets. By default, he was saying, "Racist, you were right. He was saying we are ignorant, inferior, subhuman." I was sorry to hear him say that. My sorrow deepened when no one with a voice spoke out against his position. To embrace the insults leveled by those who despise you is to become their victim indeed!

Referring to yourself in a derogatory manner is a sure sign of low self-esteem and self-hatred. When your deceivers can stand back and listen to you put yourself down, they can say, "Mission accomplished." This scenario reminds me of an old post-game NFL press conference. After a devastating loss to the Chicago Bears, the opposing NFL coach said, "The Bears are who we thought they were." Replace *Bears* with *niggas*—you get the picture now? This is how we give away our power to ascend. Rappers and comedians can apply mountains of window-dressing and reasons for using self-degrading epithets to no avail. The bottom line is that if you were not deceived, you would not find it cool or funny.

One day, we will no longer grab the low-hanging fruit to get laughs based on the pain and tragedy of racism. One day, the veil of deception will fall and fade from memory. One day, the descendants of slaves in America will hold one another in high esteem as many of their ancestors had.

In a vision one morning just before I woke, I saw a stream of young brown faces smiling and grinning from ear to ear. They were smiling to hold back the joy. They were smiling because they had been born into a generation, no longer deceived.

One day … one day. That day can't come soon enough.

NINE

Closing the Black Poverty Gap— The Time Has Come

Young people of color live under this strange dichotomy. They have natural abilities in high-tech fields, business, art and athletics, but low levels of education to prepare for the careers that follow. Foreign graduates flood into the US each year by the tens of thousands to take high-paying tech jobs under the H-1B program. These foreign young people never experience poverty in the US or live in crime-ridden neighborhoods. They will never stand in a welfare line or swipe a food-stamp card. Their ancestors never fought for freedom or defended our nation. These young visitors will walk right into the American dream because they realized the value of preparation.

Imagine a program in twenty major inner-city school districts that recruits and prepares young people of color to fill these H-1B jobs. This is just one of dozens of ways the DOS population could close the unemployment and income gaps in the US. This can be achieved only by a people who are not deceived; the deceived are already making excuses why their children can't prepare to take these solid-income careers.

Again, how deep is our love? We must exhibit a special love for the DOS. The shared heritage, sacrifice, and price that was paid to justify our existence is reason enough.

May your love for your brothers and sisters be abundant. Let your love flow when they excel and achieve—no more haters. Let your love graciously flow even when they disappoint you because we all make mistakes. Let your love flow even more when they piss you off; remember that they have been deceived and that we should have love for and patience with the deceived.

Everyone does not shake loose from the chains of deception at the same time. If it had not been for your good parents with clear vision, who knows where you might be today? You could be counted among the totally deceived among us.

The deceived among us are known by their fruit.

They will crush a child's dreams without realizing it.

They will kill their brothers over money or turf or because of a menacing glare.

They will march in the streets to raise the minimum wage but not understand they are worth so much more than the minimum.

They make excuses and blame white people for bad decisions they make every day.

They will look to government programs to provide what they must ultimately provide for themselves.

They feel better supporting the businesses of merchants who are not black.

They celebrate their children's high school graduations as if they were passports to higher learning but make no plans for postsecondary education for them.

They believe a political party can change the socioeconomic woes of black people in America but don't realize that a political party is complicit in causing those same socioeconomic woes.

The women accept inferior treatment and no respect from the men they share their beds with.

WE ARE
OUR OWN WORST
ENEMIES

They will look into the mirror and wish the image looking back at them had lighter skin or straighter hair.

They ignore the beauty and disrespect the value of the brown-skinned women.

I could go on, but you get the picture.

TEN

Speaking of Beautiful, Brown-Skinned Women—Putting the Queen Back on Her Throne

Women of color, how beautiful you are. Your unique qualities have been legendary from the days of Cleopatra to the divas of today. Your curves and edges, your intellect and attitude. Your ageless brown skin tones are delicious. You still display a youthful beauty as you gracefully age. I know it doesn't rhyme, but I have to say it correctly anyway: "You know what they say—brown don't crack."

This display of appreciation for women of color is not meant to diminish the beauty and splendor of women of all ethnicities. Our mission here is to remove deception. We must stop the madness. Many black Americans discriminate based on skin color in their own ranks. Black men and women grant preference to others with lighter skin. This practice is a form of racism. Or maybe it's the pot calling the kettle racist. This silly, stupid, and embarrassing tradition of deceived blacks must end.

If you are blessed to meet a virtuous man or woman who is interested in you in spite of your faults, the last thing on your mind should be how dark his or her skin is. There might be something to the old proverb, "The darker the berry, the sweeter the juice."

Now let's get back to the point, my beautiful brown queens. We know European women spend billions each year on tanning creams and salons, collagen lip injections, wrinkle removers, and butt lifts all to get what comes naturally to you. Your beauty is legendary and established, so why don't you demand royal treatment? You deserve it.

Low self-esteem seems to be pervasive among low-income, brown-skinned women, and that has huge ripple effects throughout inner-city America. It works like this. A sister with low self-esteem shares a bed with a guy who has no future interest in her. Looking for love, she labors under the false premise that a piece of a man is better than none at all. The night is over, and the piece of man is gone, but he left his something behind. The deposit has been made, and she will have to deal with it alone.

This scenario is played out in the 'hood thousands of times each night across America. The result is a 70 percent out-of-wedlock birthrate, and that is just the tip of the iceberg. A disproportionate number of these male children grow up to participate in the carnage that we refer to as inner-city violence.

The result of sleeping with men who have no future commitment to them or any offspring contributes to the carnage. Our women must demand much more from the men they share their beds with. In most cases, our young women are totally unprepared to deal with parenthood alone. The financial implications are obvious, but the emotional trauma the children endure is not.

I have been involved with a mentoring program that targets inner-city boys who often display two life-limiting characteristics. Most of these young men display an unusual amount of anger but lack any conflict-resolution thought processes. When I am successful in getting them to be open and honest about their anger, it is often directed toward their mothers. They love their mothers but hold them in great disdain simultaneously. They subconsciously blame their mothers for the lack of fathers in their homes. The mothers are also held in contempt for having too many male callers who don't care about them. These young men conclude that the men want their mother for only one thing. It is not uncommon for a boy to explode into a fit of rage stating that he hates his mother acting like a "ho'." This anger combined with a lack of conflict-resolution skills breed contempt that spills onto the streets.

The lack of appreciation for preparation is the second characteristic that is equally as negative. The guys think that life will just happen and that they have no control over the decision-making process. These boys have never heard the old saying "Failure to plan is planning to fail."

The majority of inner-city single moms are too busy with their own drama to even notice that their children have no dreams or aspirations. Children with no dreams are truly in poverty. People with no dreams see no future and thus have no sense of self-control. Young men with no self-control will pull the trigger. In their minds, they have no future to ruin.

Blacks operating under this deception commit more than 50 percent of the murders in the US. Most of our deceived single mothers in the 'hood can't rise to the challenge of properly mentoring their boys. These two disturbing facts are morbidly connected; one statistic feeds the other.

Growing up in the 'hood can be brutal. I recall gunfire and ducking for cover as I walked home from school on more than one occasion. When I was fourteen, a boy I didn't know had been trapped in an isolated corridor at school by a gang of punks. The attack on this boy stemmed most likely from an incident that had occurred the previous day. I could tell that because the punks were wearing brogan boots, and they were not wearing them for style. These boots sometimes come with steel toes to inflict maximum damage.

I saw the helpless boy surrounded and punched until he hit the ground. He lay on the floor in the fetal position in a vain effort to protect his vital parts. He endured an onslaught of kicks until someone yelled, "Here comes security." That day, I made a vow that if I ever received such a beatdown and survived, I would kill everyone involved.

Operating under deception, we have created a vicious circle. I was in danger of becoming a cog in the killing machine myself. In the absence of strong fatherly guidance, the violence is perpetuated.

Boys subconsciously crave direction and discipline from their fathers. I never told my mother what I had witnessed, and I never told her of my vow. It just didn't seem right to discuss this matter with her;

after all, she was a girl. The beatdown and my planned response was man's business. But I was blessed to have dad around for most of my childhood.

The shooters responsible for the murder rate in Chicago paint a clear picture of life in some single-mother households. The black deception has reduced the parental status of many beautiful, brown-skinned women to a level that could be referred to as killer breeders.

My deceived sisters, this insanity must stop! You must place a higher value on yourself and your bed privileges. The most ironic part of this dilemma is that good things happen when you reject guys who have no interest in you beyond your crotch. The hit-it-and-quit-it guys have no patience, and they will leave you alone.

And once they are out of the picture, the men with the potential to commit can then find you. You must stop making babies and depriving them of the fathers they need and deserve. Yes, you deprive them by making bad choices in your bedroom. The bad decision is where the deprivation begins.

Hold your head high! Realize the value of the fire and beauty you possess. If he has no career plans, no realistic future dreams, no true commitment to you, "He can't get none." End of story.

ELEVEN

People Who Can Bond Can Rise

T hey redlined your parents, but your parents still maintained a higher homeownership rate than today's deceived generations. Homeownership should not be an option. After you have become an expert in some field, your next priority should be to own a home.

The time has come for us to end the insane practice of building other people's wealth while we stagnate in financial obscurity. Stop renting. Yes, I said it—stop renting. If you can't put together a full down payment, don't let that stop you. Use your imagination. Let your creative juices flow. Just don't settle for renting. Work part time for a year and save. Borrow from relatives who love you. Partner with another family. If two families come together and purchase a single, good-sized property, that's better than two families renting. The two families can build equity that benefits them both, while renting benefits only your landlord.

One family lives upstairs and the other family lives in the remodeled basement. This arrangement is far better than renting. Buy in an up-and-coming neighborhood and eventually the equity can be leveraged into a down payment on a second house for the basement family.

I know, I know—this level of love, trust, cooperation, and sacrifice is not common among blacks, but that's because they have been deceived. The DOS must love and forgive everyone. Nelson Mandela, who fought racism on an elite level, said, "Holding hate and unforgiveness is the same as drinking poison and hoping it will kill your enemy." Mandela refused to give in to hate and deception, and he rose from prisoner to president. Love all people, but have a special love for the DOS.

Do not be afraid to partner with good people to start or expand a business. Combine your resources. Buy income property. Expand your income sources above and beyond your job. Your ancestors gave you the willpower and determination to excel and create. The time has come for you to reach down inside and tap the potential that sleeps within you.

We should display this special love for one another because of our common ancestors and our common struggle. The deception divides us; it sows seeds of distrust among us. When we begin to display this special love, that's a sure sign the cloak of deception is fading.

There are many creative paths to homeownership; use your imagination. Stop renting. Reject low-income housing and all other long-term government programs. The creators of these programs might have had good intentions, but is it your intention to remain in poverty as a needy, low-income person? If your answer isn't "Hell no!" shame on you. This is why you must reject government poverty programs today in your heart and mind and future plans. There is no shame in using these programs as stepping stones, as shovels to dig your way out. The shame is in being deceived into believing that this is your permanent way of life and that you are powerless to change it.

DOS parents, I am speaking to you directly. Single moms, your job is more challenging. Your beautiful brown children didn't choose to put you in this challenging situation; your bad decision-making skills did that.

Nevertheless, you must love education. You must become an education samurai parent. Starting from your children's birth, prepare yourself and your surroundings to become learning environments. You brought them into this world, so it's your responsibility to see that they are not deceived into believing they are underachievers.

Free from the cloak of deception, your children will excel in school. Accept or give no excuses for less-than-excellent academic performance. Provide discipline and structure that is conducive to learning. Make rules based on common sense. As soon as your children get home from school, they should complete their homework and do their chores. If they do not have homework, they can complete a backup assignment you have already laid out. Inspect your children's homework for quality and accuracy. No cell phones, games, TV, or computers until all work and chores are completed. Offer great rewards for good work and dire consequences for poor-quality work.

A brilliant college professor shared a human behavior rule that is true: "In the absence of dire consequences for poor performance, performance will always decline." I have managed dozens of businesses and thousands of employees in my life, and I have been intimately involved with the raising of seven children. Those experiences have taught me that the professor was correct; his statement is true in the workplace, as well as at home.

We have always used some form of what I call the samurai-education philosophy in our household. All of these children attended college and we have attended numerous graduation ceremonies. Two are still working toward post-graduate degrees. The samurai-education philosophy works because what you feed the most becomes the strongest in you. Feed your children's love and thirst for reading and learning. Inspire them with stories of the great achievements and innovations of our ancestors. Own it as if Granville T. Woods or Frederick Jones were your great, great uncle. Who knows? Either might have been. Our ancestral records were not high-priority items in times past.

We as a people must regain the swagger of academic excellence. Cultivating a spirit of aspiration and achievement in our children is not the responsibility of the school system or the government; it is our responsibility.

If your child has high aspirations and achievements, you have done a great job. If your child has little or no aspirations and low achievement, do not blame the school system. These are our dear children; they do not belong to the government.

TWELVE

Take the Oath

This book has revealed many inconvenient truths concerning our ancestors, our country, and our future. We have explored why things are as they are and what must happen to change the future.

Our ancestors had strong moral character and a powerful sense of community. They were great thinkers, innovators, and businesspeople. They were determined to never give up the hope of freedom. Once they were free, they prospered and performed as well as, or even better than any other ethnic group in America, in spite of the post–Civil War Democrats' attempts to block their path to prosperity by any means necessary.

Our country failed to enforce its Constitution and protect its citizens from domestic terror campaigns, and those failures cost the brown-skinned DOS untold billions by the theft of intellectual property and other lost economic opportunities. Nonetheless, we have a God-given ability to excel in this capitalist society. The deception that has blocked our path is well within our power to remove.

You can become samurai parents whose children set the academic standards for the nation. Your children can become a new wave of tech entrepreneurs. They can dominate in sports, entertainment, and business on a higher level than anyone imagined.

But before we can become the super-achievers we were destined to be, we must strip ourselves of the black deception and distance ourselves from all its egregious connotations.

The veil is beginning to lift. Many brown-skinned people are speaking out in confidence. The shadow of the victim mentality is beginning to fade in the sunshine of the truth.

Taraji P. Henson said, "If you have to walk across that college graduation stage with your child on your hip, do it!" Do not allow a child born early in your life to keep you from your destiny. Morgan Freeman spoke about how his strong work ethic got him into the position he holds today. The interviewer responded with, "But Morgan, not everybody can do that." Freeman paused for a brief moment before rendering this classic response: "Bullsh@#*! Of course they can!"

In the early 1900s, Marcus Garvey said, "Never forget that intelligence rules the world and ignorance carries its burden. Therefore, remove yourself as far as possible from ignorance and seek to be intelligent." If only the DOS had heard his words.

People of color, DOS, African-Americans, nonimmigrants—whatever you care to call us—are showing signs of waking up from the drowsy fog of victimhood that has robbed so many of confidence and hope. We are what we see ourselves to be in our hearts. That truth written thousands of years ago is still the truth. If you see yourself as a victim, you are one. If you see yourself as a victor, you are one. This, my friend, is why the deception must end. We must see ourselves as the determined, undefeatable masters of our destinies.

You have now studied the history. You have learned the facts in this sacred manual. Embrace the prescription, and let the medicine heal you. Share it with all who need it. Your failure to get well is a surrender to the racists. You might as well say, "You win! We give up! You were right. We are inferior."

Now is your moment of truth, so take the oath.

1. I will never consider myself a victim; I will consider myself the master of my destiny.
2. I reject labels of all kinds. I reserve the right and responsibility to define myself.
3. I will prepare myself for success by working to become an expert in some field whether in business, arts, sports, entertainment, or humanitarian outreach regardless of my age or condition.
4. I forgive every person who has or will do me harm. I hate no one. I will remember that harboring hate and unforgiveness only harms me, not my enemies. I will remember that living with hate and unforgiveness is like drinking poison while hoping it will kill my enemy.
5. I reject all long-term government social programs such as welfare, food stamps, low-income housing, and the like. I am an extraordinary individual fully capable of competing in a capitalist society. If I ever use a social safety net, it will be to help me train and prepare for a better future. I will work toward the day that I can reject such programs as they are not good enough for my family.
6. I refuse to allow drugs, alcohol, or any other harmful vice ruin my life.
7. I will nourish my mind and body with good things and positive thoughts.
8. I will make necessary adjustments in my social circle for my greater good.
9. I will encourage all my family and friends (see Legacy Page) to discover their true destinies. I will patiently teach and encourage them to untangle the black deception.

I ask all who dare to respond to this challenge of love to learn lessons and teach them to others. Write the names of seven people you will make it your responsibility to teach this to. Your responsibility is to undeceive them. Go to the Legacy Page and love seven people enough to share the truth with them. If they don't read, read it to them, get them the audio book—whatever it takes.

The lightbulb gets brighter when you write down the names of seven souls whom you might guide out of deception into the truth, out of mental poverty into enlightenment. You, my friend, are no longer on the problem side of the equation. You have transmogrified into the solution. At the end of the day, you can say, "I led seven more people out of the darkness of *The Black Deception.*"

My Legacy

Congratulations
You are no longer
DECiEVED!

Glossary

Epithet: a disparaging or abusive word, as in a racial slur.

Impunity: exempt from punishment, freedom from the consequences of bad action.

Schema: a cognitive system which helps us organize and make sense of information, once retained and organized, schema influences your actions and relationship with the subject of that information. Example, you have heard all of your life that snakes are dangerous and that they will bite, you now take action to avoid snakes at all cost, and you are drawn to information that supports your theory and you resist information to the contrary. Schemas influence how we see others and the world in general, it can also hinder our ability to accept truth when it does not fit our mental framework.

Abdication: failure to fulfill ones duty or responsibility, to renounce office

Aberrant: deviant, as in behavior, atypical, abnormal

Dogma: a fixed position of belief from an authority, accepted without question

Eclectic: ideas from various sources, a mixture of what appears to be the best

Egregious: extraordinary in a bad way, flagrantly bad, offensive behavior

Eschew: to abstain from, avoid, or to shun an idea or concept

Gregarious: found of company, outgoing, friendly, sociable

Interrogatories: a written question put to one party by another party,

Introspection: the examination of one's own thoughts, feelings and actions

Paradigm: /pere dim/ a model, template or example of how it should be

Voluminous: large in size and capacity

Transmogrified: changed in a surprising or magical manner, to a new shape or outlook superior to the old one.

www.ingramcontent.com/pod-product-compliance
Lightning Source LLC
Chambersburg PA
CBHW030529290526
45786CB00004B/1662